Girls with their ox-drawn wagon head West. Because of their strength and stamina, oxen were often used to haul the westbound wagons.

Cornerstones of Freedom

The Story of
WOMEN
WHO SHAPED
THE WEST

By Mary Virginia Fox

CHILDRENS PRESS®
CHICAGO

Employees of Canada's Hudson's Bay Company traded with the Indians for furs.

Library of Congress Cataloging-in-Publication Data

Fox, Mary Virginia.

    The story of women who shaped the West / by Mary Virginia Fox.
      p.   cm. — (Cornerstones of freedom)
    Summary: Presents examples of women who helped to shape the Western frontier in such diverse roles as schoolteacher, missionary, justice of the peace, and homesteader.
    ISBN 0-516-04757-4
    1. Women pioneers—West (U.S.)—History—Juvenile literature. 2. West (U.S.)—History—Juvenile literature. 3. Frontier and pioneer life—West (U.S.)—Juvenile literature. [1. Women pioneers. 2. Pioneers. 3. West (U.S.)—History. 4. Frontier and pioneer life—West (U.S.)] I. Title. II. Series.
F596.F63   1991
978′.02′0922—dc20   90-21444
                                  CIP
                                    AC

PHOTO CREDITS

The Bettmann Archive—5, 6, (left), 19 (right), 30 (2 photos) 31, (3 photos), 32

Culver Pictures—1, 4, 6 (right), 28 (left)

Historical Pictures Service, Chicago—11, 18, 19 (left & center), 22 (left)

Kansas State Historical Society, Topeka, Kansas—26 (2 photos)

Courtesy of King Ranch Archives—13 (2 photos), 15 (left), 16 (2 photos); © Paulus Lesser, 14

North Wind Picture Archives—2, 8, 17, 21, 22 (right), 29 (right)

Oregon Historical Society—7 (left) [Neg #CN 002989], 7 (right) [Neg #ORHI 85863], 9 [Neg #ORHI 11781]

SuperStock International, Inc.—© Augusts Upitis, 15 (right)

UPI/Bettmann Newsphotos—27 (top & bottom right), 28 (right), 29 (left)

USC Library Department of Special Collections, California Historical Society/Title Insurance & Trust Co. (L.A.) Collection of Historical Photographs—24

Wyoming State Museum—Cover, 25 (2 photos), 27 (left); © W.H. Jackson, 25 (right)

(Cover—Ella Martfeld homesteading 1910-1912)

Explorers, trappers, and miners were the first European men to cross the plains and mountains of the West, but women were soon to follow. The women were nurses and teachers, homesteaders and peddlers, horse traders and madams, reformers and ranch hands. They knew the dangers they faced.

Utah settlers pose in front of a log cabin in 1875.

In many cases, it was women who suffered most. There were the hazards of giving birth and raising children with no medical care. There was the social isolation that could bring numbing loneliness. But without these women, the West would never have developed as it did. Men blazed the trails, but when women and children went West, the commitment was made, and the settlement was home.

Narcissa Prentiss Whitman

Marcus Whitman

Every woman had her own reasons for braving such harsh conditions. Some were wives and mothers who dreamed of a better life for their families. Some were single women who hoped for the independence denied to them elsewhere. Some wanted to carry the Christian gospel to the Indians. Narcissa Prentiss was only sixteen when she offered her services to the Presbyterian Mission Board. She wanted to bring her Christian faith to the Indians of the West. The church, however, was not about to permit a young unmarried woman to travel alone in the wilderness. And so Narcissa had a long wait.

Finally, when she was twenty-seven, she met a man who shared her dreams. Marcus Whitman was a medical doctor as well as a preacher, and his services were sorely needed in the West. The two were criticized as "meddlesome do-gooders" and people around them tried to discourage them. However, this opposition made Narcissa and Marcus even more determined to put "their lives in God's hands." They were married on February 18, 1836, and immediately made plans to head West to the end of the Oregon Trail. No white woman had ever made such a trip. They tried to encourage others to go with them, but only one couple would join them— Henry Harmon Spalding and his wife Eliza. Both couples planned to preach the gospel to whomever would listen.

Eliza Spalding (left) with two young children. Henry Harmon Spalding (right)

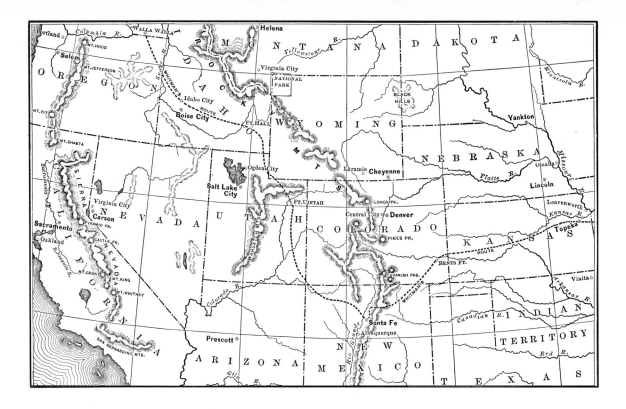

They traveled from Pennsylvania to St. Louis by stagecoach and then took a steamboat up the Missouri River to Liberty. There, they gathered their supplies and bought wagons. Against the advice of trappers who knew the trail, Whitman also bought twelve horses, six mules, and seventeen head of cattle.

The way West was hard from the start. Blinding dust storms alternated with torrential rains that mired the wagons. They slept in tents that Narcissa had made out of oiled bed ticking. Her clothing turned out to be quite unsuitable, but Narcissa had her eastern ways, and the only thing she would change was her shoes—she switched to men's heavy boots.

Little by little, they had to abandon their equipment on the trail. They kept their wagons as long as they could, often lowering them by ropes over steep cliffs. When the last axle splintered, they saved the best two wheels and made a cart to carry what possessions remained.

The Whitmans' journey was made even more trying by the constant complaining of the Spaldings. The rivalry and friction between the two families reached such a point that they decided to split forces as soon as they reached a likely spot for their missionary work. So the Spaldings settled among the Nez Percé Indians at Lapwai in what is now Idaho,

The Spaldings established this mission at the junction of Lapwai Creek and the Clearwater River in Idaho.

and the Whitmans went to Waiilatpu to live among the Cayuse.

When word got back to the East that two women had made the trip unharmed and a doctor had set up a practice in the wilds of Oregon, many other families began planning their own trip west to settle the frontier.

The Whitmans built a modest home, and Narcissa—true to her eastern ways—enjoyed serving tea to visitors, whether they were trappers or Indians. And soon she was hostess to other families who followed in their footsteps.

For eleven years, Marcus and Narcissa ministered to the sick and preached the word of God. In time, they established a school for the settlers' children. It was a hard and often grueling life, but one that seemed to gratify them both.

Everything came to an abrupt end when the Cayuse tribe caught measles from passing emigrants. More than half of them died, and the survivors became convinced that the sickness was a white man's plot to kill all Indians. On November 29, 1847, a Cayuse warrior named Tamahas sought revenge on the Whitmans and led a raid on the mission. Marcus, Narcissa, and twelve other settlers were killed in that raid.

An artist's portrayal of the assassination of Marcus Whitman

The remaining settlers raised an army and drove the Cayuse people from their land. Joe Meek, whose daughter had died in the massacre, left for Washington with the tragic news and a demand that Congress pass a bill creating the Territory of Oregon. Soon a governor and United States marshal were appointed to keep order. The Whitmans died in the last Indian uprising in that part of the West.

Eventually a statue was erected in honor of Narcissa Prentiss Whitman—the first white woman to settle in Oregon, tea parties and all—whose courage and compassion inspired so many others.

In another corner of the West, Henrietta Chamberlain King lived through almost every important chapter of Texas history. She survived war with Indians, war with Mexicans, and war with Union forces. She saw the cattle boom, the coming of the railroad, and the discovery of oil. And Henrietta King had a hand in shaping many of the changes.

Henrietta was teaching school in Brownsville, Texas, when she met Richard King, a riverboat captain. He decided land would bring a better profit. Although his friends thought him foolish, Richard began to buy up vast tracts of land for very little money. Then he purchased cattle from Mexico to put the land to use.

The Captain, as he was always called, shared his big dreams for the future with the well-educated young schoolteacher. Henrietta may have thought some of his plans were unrealistic, but she had fallen in love and his home would be her home.

They were married in December 1854, and Captain King purchased a stagecoach for their four-day trip to his Santa Gertrudis ranch. Armed outriders kept pace with the coach during the day and stood watch over the camp at night to guard against Indians and Mexican bandits, who often took lives as well as loot in these parts.

Unfortunately, the land King had described in

Left: Captain Richard King. Right: Henrietta King (center) surrounded by her family

such glowing terms had been scorched by a drought. The grass had shriveled and died. The mud of the watering sinks had turned to white dust. The "house" he had described with such excitement was a small three-room shelter. But to Henrietta, the Captain's enthusiasm made everything seem right.

From the start, she was a partner-manager with her husband, riding the range with the Captain.

Together they raised five children, and the small shelter was replaced by a stately mansion. In 1863, during the Civil War, Union forces captured Brownsville and set out for the ranch to capture the rebel Richard King. He escaped, but Henrietta, seven months pregnant, remained behind and saw her guard murdered and her home plundered.

When the war was over, drought and a drop in the

The first King home at the Santa Gertrudis ranch was constructed in 1859.

price of cattle brought hard times to the King ranch. When the Captain died in 1885, Henrietta inherited a tremendous financial debt along with the land.

With characteristic determination, she proceeded to put her accounts in order. She had the help of her son-in-law Robert Kleberg, but it was Henrietta's vision and Henrietta's decisions that changed the way cattle were handled on the King ranch.

Abandoning the old cattle drives her husband had so loved, she put a rail line through her property so that cattle could be shipped to market—with a marked decrease in loss of animals. Then she planned a new town—called Kingsville—as the main shipping center. She donated money for churches and a

Henrietta King brought water to the ranch with artesian wells (left). Santa Gertrudis cattle (above) are a cross between Brahmins and Shorthorns.

school, and kept saloons out. Many families wanted to settle in Kingsville. Henrietta owned and operated the town's lumber company, weekly newspaper, and cotton gin.

She found new ways to bring water to the land. Well-drilling equipment was brought in, and artesian water from deep underground saved the livestock on her ranch during a devastating drought.

Richard King had bred cavalry horses, police horses, and workhorses. Henrietta and her son-in-law began developing racehorses and bred three Kentucky Derby winners. Their most successful breeding venture, however, was the Santa Gertrudis strain of cattle, noted for their resistance to disease and their ability to thrive in harsh climates.

Henrietta King (left) in 1905. By the 1930s, the main house at the King ranch was a stately mansion (right).

Henrietta King had inherited a half-million acres of land and a half-million-dollar debt. When she died, she left an estate of $5.4 million and more than a million acres of land. And her efforts continued to reap dividends. Oil was discovered on the King property and much of the money was reinvested in land — a lesson learned from the Captain. Within the last few decades, the boundaries of the King ranch have spread to Australia, Venezuela, and Brazil. Henrietta would have been proud.

Many women with humbler life-styles also made their mark on the West. In 1856, Carrie Roach

Many homesteaders who headed West in wagons piled high with furniture and household goods were forced to abandon their treasures along the way.

joined a wagon train with a minimum of supplies—and no husband by her side.

Carrie had learned to shoot a gun as well as put food in a pot. She had seed for planting and a plow to break ground. She also had Angus—a sway-backed mule bought with the last of her money. In her trunk she had one long coat, an extra set of "under things," and wool and flax to spin and weave into clothing.

Carrie settled in a less than choice spot in Nebraska, because Angus could go no farther, and she had a fever herself. She waved good-bye to the wagon train and set about making her camp. Along the way, she had seen strange knobs on the horizon

The prairie grasses held the soil tight with their long, matted roots. This sod could be cut into building blocks for houses.

that turned out to be shelters made of mud and prairie grass. Without trees to build a proper house, Carrie soon realized that a sod house was the only alternative. So, with nothing more than a shovel and a hunting knife, she built her own sod house and planted seed. Soon she had grown enough vegetables to trade with passing wagons.

The first winter was the worst for Carrie Roach. For months she saw no one and the wind never stopped blowing. But Carrie seemed to have a knack for survival, learning quickly and inventing her own solutions to problems.

In time, neighbors settled within sight. Carrie was always glad to pass on the lessons she had learned from that first bleak winter when the wind never stopped blowing.

Carrie Roach never married, but her small house was often full of children who loved to hear her stories. Carrie had a way with words. If she could have put those words on paper, it would have been the story of many brave women of the West.

By contrast, Jessie Ann Benton was born into a family of wealth and education. Her father was Thomas Hart Benton, the famous senator from Missouri. Benton's interest in the West brought the family in contact with many scientists and explorers, and early in 1840, Jessie met Lieutenant John Charles Fremont, of the U.S. army's Topographical Corps. Fremont's first job was to map the Dakota country—the beginning of his career and the beginning of a strong love between Fremont and Jessie.

Thomas Hart Benton

Jessie Benton Fremont

John Charles Fremont

After the two were married on October 19, 1841, Jessie took a keen interest in planning Fremont's expeditions, but the army did not allow her to accompany him. The expeditions were made to encourage migration by finding the best routes West and the most desirable areas for settlement.

When Fremont returned in August 1844 from a successful journey to Oregon and California, Jessie went with her husband to Washington, D.C., where he gave a detailed account of his findings to President Polk. But it was Jessie herself who transformed the dry details of mapping into a highly readable and informative report that was later published in a commercial edition. Her report, said to have "exercised a greater influence upon Far Western settlement than any other single book," was carried by almost every pioneer heading West.

In 1849, Jessie finally had a chance to see the land she had written about. Her first trip was made by ship, from New York to Panama, by land across the isthmus, and then by sailboat along the coast to Monterey, California, where the Fremonts built their first home. Later, when Fremont invested in mining property near Mariposa, Jessie got a taste of what primitive frontier life was really like.

Fremont continued to map the West, searching for a southern railroad route to the Pacific. During

Members of Fremont's expedition planted the U.S. flag
in the Colorado Rockies.

his absences Jessie made frequent trips east to see
her father. Her literary talents and her knowledge
of languages brought her into contact with many
members of the United States government, includ-
ing the president. She fully supported her husband's
role in the 1846 revolt against Mexican rule in
California.

When California was made part of the United

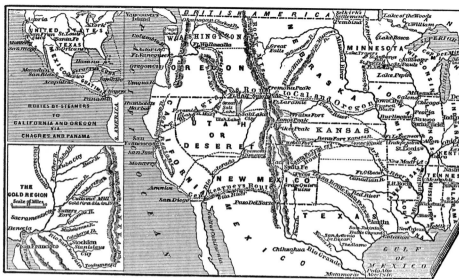

John Charles Fremont explored the West on expeditions ranging from the upper Mississippi to California. Jessie Benton Fremont (left) wrote about her husband's adventures.

States, John Charles Fremont was elected senator from that state. In 1856, he ran as the first Republican candidate for president of the United States, and Jessie took an active role in the campaign.

Although her husband was defeated and financial difficulties left them almost penniless, Jessie was not discouraged. She wrote a series of articles for the *Atlantic Monthly* that were later published in book form. She also wrote fiction, but Jessie's personal memoirs and her enthusiasm for the West were her most important legacy.

Jessie Fremont had access to some of the most

important officials in the American government, but there were other women who wielded great influence at the grass-roots level. For example, Esther Morris's tea party in her log-cabin home in South Pass City, Wyoming, had far-reaching effects on the status of women throughout the world. It was August 1869, and the men of Carter County were about to choose their representative to the first Wyoming Territorial Legislature.

Among the dozen or so people invited to the tea party were the two opposing candidates for the legislature. Esther urged that the successful candidate promise to work for the passage of an act granting women the right to vote in the new territory. Both men pledged their support.

Colonel William H. Bright, a Democrat, was elected, and he drafted a bill that would give women not only the right to vote but also the right to hold public office. The bill was passed, and it made international news. Women of Great Britain cabled congratulations, and the King of Prussia sent word to President Grant that the bill showed "evidence of progress and enlightenment and civil liberty in America."

Soon, other bills protected and upgraded the status of women. They could now own property in

Under the Homestead Act, citizens would receive title to land if they lived and worked on it. Here, a woman homesteader receives the deed to her land.

their own name, earn money—and keep it—for the first time in history, and retain guardianship of their minor children if they were widowed.

Women made up only one-sixth of the population of the wilderness territory of Wyoming, but those women had endured hardships and shouldered responsibilities as well as any man. It was only justice that they should have an equal say about their government. Women were often more inclined to stand for law and order and for decency in moral standards. If the West were tamed, women would have a hand in it.

24

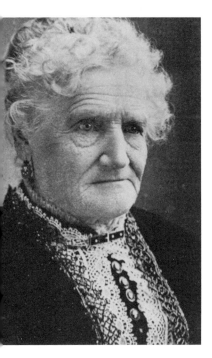

Esther Morris

South Pass City, Wyoming in 1870

Meanwhile, in South Pass City, Esther Morris was appointed the first woman Justice of the Peace in the United States. The day she was sworn in, John Morris, a local saloon keeper—and husband of the new justice—objected to his wife's accepting the office and made a scene in the courtroom. Esther Morris promptly fined him for contempt of court and, when he refused to pay his fine, she sent him to jail. This did not break up the marriage, however, and Esther continued to mete out justice. An attorney who practiced before her court said, "She showed no mercy, but her decisions were always just."

Western states continued to pass record-setting legislation. Wyoming was the first state to grant

Argonia 4/6 '87

Mrs Salter.

Argonia

Madam

You are hereby notified that at an ele[ction]
held in the city of Argonia on Monday April 4, '87, for [the]
purpose of electing city officers, you were duly el[ected]
to the office of Mayor of said city, you will take
notice thereof and govern yourself accordingly.

Wm H Watson Ma[yor]
F. A. Ruse Clerk. [?]

Susanna Salter (left) received this official notice of her
election as mayor of Argonia, Kansas, in 1887.

women the right to vote, but Utah, Colorado, and
Idaho followed shortly. Argonia, Kansas, elected the
first woman mayor in the United States in 1887
when Mrs. Susanna Medora Salter campaigned
without much opposition. The following year, Mrs.
Mary Lowman was elected mayor of Oskaloosa,
Kansas, and all five seats on the town council went
to women too.

In 1955, the Wyoming legislature chose Esther
Hobart Morris as the person whose statue should fill
the state's niche in Statuary Hall in the Capitol
building in Washington, D.C.

The Esther Hobart Morris statue in Statuary Hall (above). Nellie Tayloe Ross (top right) signs the oath of office as Wyoming's governor. Jeannette Rankin (right, in center), the first woman to serve in the House of Representatives, believed that war was stupid and cruel.

Other "firsts" included Wyoming's woman governor, Nellie Tayloe Ross, elected in 1925. She later became the first woman director of the U.S. mint. In 1916, Jeannette Rankin, a well-known pacifist, was elected to the House of Representatives from the state of Montana.

Annie Oakley (left). Annie (right) trick-shooting over the shoulder

Annie Oakley is probably one of the best-known figures of the Old West, but her professional performances as a sharpshooter gave the public only a glamorized glimpse of female courage and talent.

Annie's early years were lived no farther west than Cincinnati. When she was nine, her father died and Annie was sent to an orphanage. Later, she was able to rejoin her mother, and she went to live on her stepfather's farm near Cincinnati, where she learned to ride a horse and shoot quail and rabbits.

At fifteen Annie entered a shooting match against Frank Butler, a professional marksman. Annie won the match—and Butler's admiration. The two were married on June 22, 1876.

The couple formed a team that traveled the Mid-

Annie Oakley (left) shot at moving targets in her appearances with Buffalo Bill's Wild West and Congress of Rough Riders of the World.

western vaudeville circuits, and Annie became famous. She joined Buffalo Bill Cody's Wild West show. Less than five feet tall and weighing under a hundred pounds, she wore fringed skirts and embroidered blouses and a wide-brimmed felt hat. She began her show by running into the ring, picking up her gun, and shattering glass balls in midair. Then, mounting a spotted pony, she snatched a pistol from the ground and smashed targets thrown by a cowboy rider. For the finale, she stood on a galloping horse and shot the flames off a revolving wheel of candles. In one of her acts, Annie flipped a playing card into the air and perforated it with bullets as it fell. Thus any repeatedly punched ticket became known as an "Annie Oakley."

During her lifetime, Annie toured the world and met the crowned heads of Europe. Only after she was injured in a railroad accident did she give up her stage career. Annie's performance may have been a caricature of Western reality, but it fired the imagination of the world. She seemed to personify the bravery, daring, and skill of frontier women. The women who really shaped the West were the women who taught school, plowed fields, doctored, carried supplies, preached the gospel, wielded a miner's pick, and raised families.

After the rugged trip West in covered wagons, pioneer women faced further hardships keeping house on the plains. Glass windows were a luxury shipped from the East on freight wagons.

A pioneer woman gathers buffalo chips for fuel. The dried buffalo droppings were the only fuel available on the treeless plains.

INDEX

ABOUT THE AUTHOR

Mary Virginia Fox was graduated from Northwestern University in Evanston, Illinois, and now lives near Madison, Wisconsin, located across the lake from the state capitol and the University of Wisconsin. She is the author of more than two dozen books for young adults and has had a number of articles published in adult publications.

Mrs. Fox and her husband have lived overseas for several months at a time and enjoy traveling. She considers herself a professional writer and an amateur artist.